WEDDING Classics

FOR ORGAN

ISBN 978-1-4768-8956-6

Shawnee Press

EXCLUSIVELY DISTRIBUTED BY

HAL•LEONARD®
CORPORATION

7777 W. BLUEMOUND RD. P.O. BOX 13819 MILWAUKEE, WI 53213

In Australia Contact:
Hal Leonard Australia Pty. Ltd.
4 Lentara Court
Cheltenham, Victoria, 3192 Australia
Email: ausadmin@halleonard.com.au

Visit Shawnee Press Online at
www.shawneepress.com

Visit Hal Leonard Online at
www.halleonard.com

Air
from WATER MUSIC

Electronic Organs

Upper: Flutes (or Tibias) 16′, 8′, 4′, 2′
Lower: Flutes 8′, 4′, Diapason 8′
Pedal: 16′, 8′
Vib./Trem.: Off

Drawbar Organs

Upper: 80 6606 000
Lower: (00) 8540 000
Pedal: 67
Vib./Trem.: Off

By GEORGE FRIDERIC HANDEL

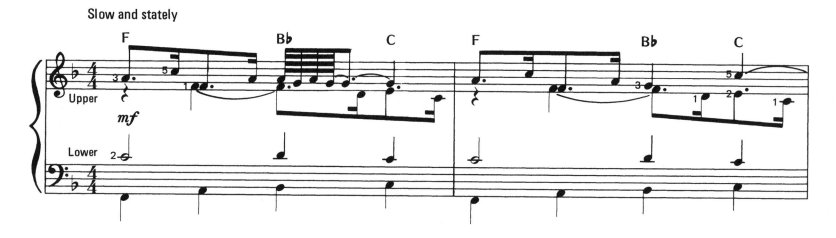

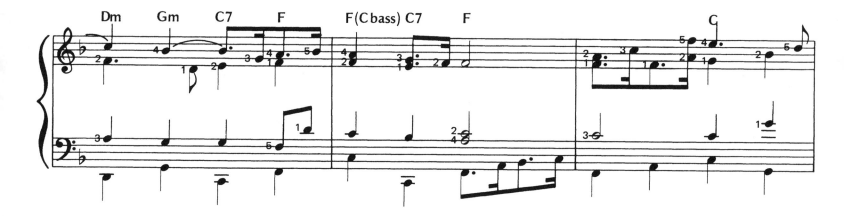

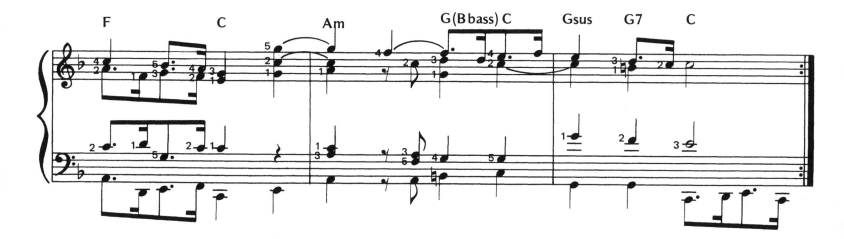

3

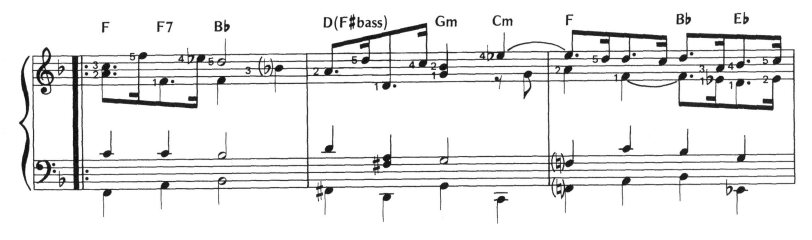

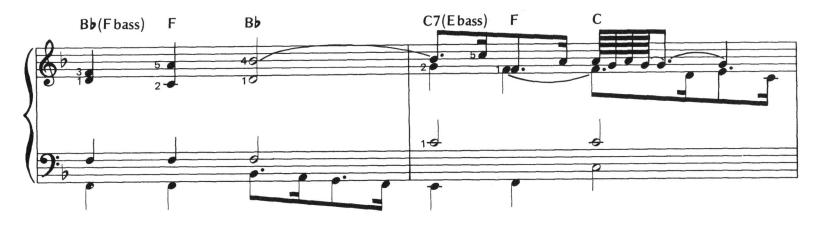

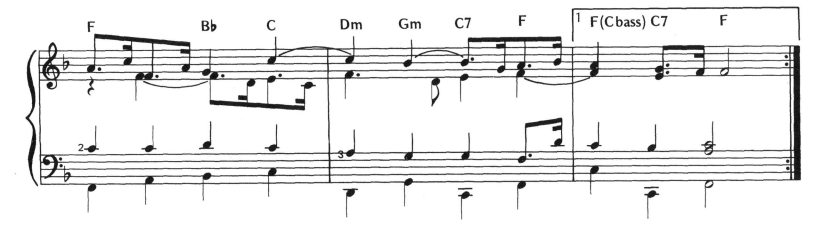

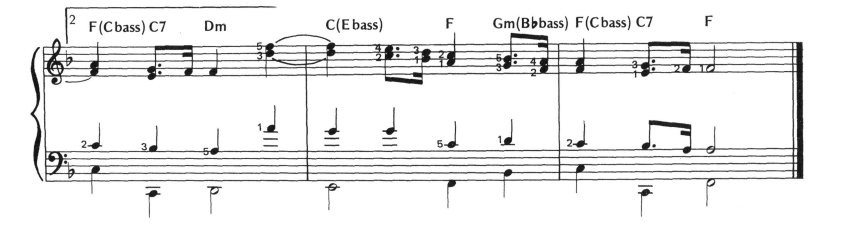

Allegro maestoso

from WATER MUSIC

Upper: *mf*
Lower: *f*
Pedal: *f*

By GEORGE FRIDERIC HANDEL

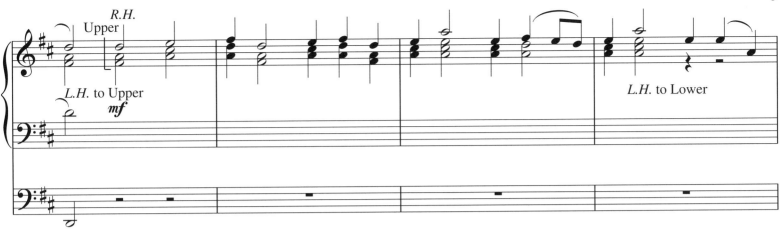

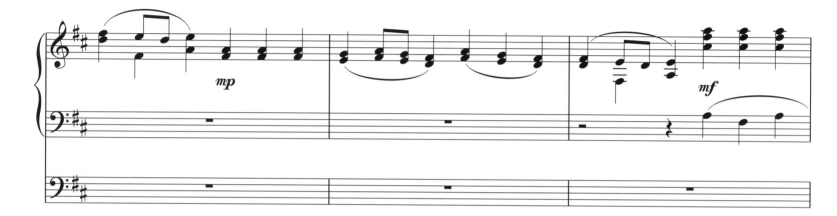

Alleluia
from EXSULTATE, JUBILATE

Upper: *p*
Lower: *f*
Pedal: *f*

By WOLFGANG AMADEUS MOZART

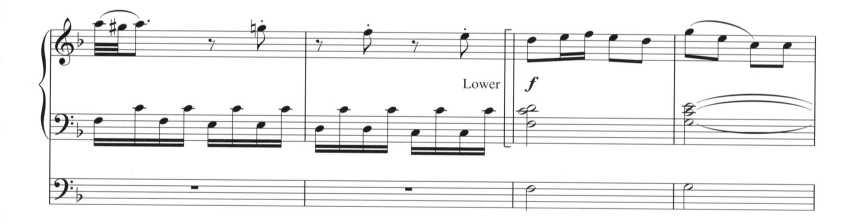

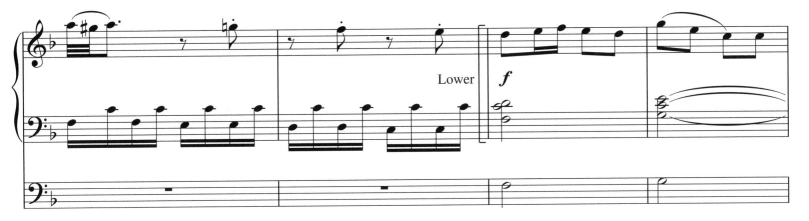

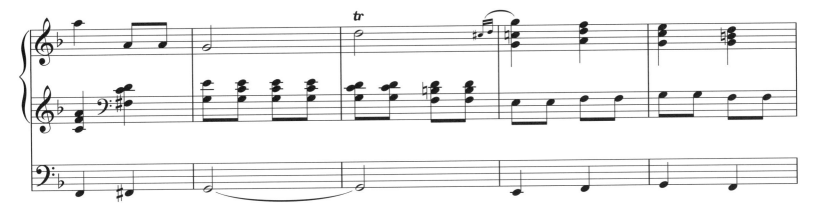

Ave Maria

Electronic and Pipe Organs

Upper: Clarinet 8', Fls. 16', 8', 4', Stg. 8'
Lower: Stg. Diap. 8'
Pedal: Soft 16'

Drawbar Organs

Upper: 52 5725 400 (00)
Lower: (00) 4454 321 (0)
Pedal: 4 (0) 2 (0) (Spinet 3)

By CHARLES GOUNOD
based on "Prelude in C Major" by JOHANN SEBASTIAN BACH

Andante moderato con moto

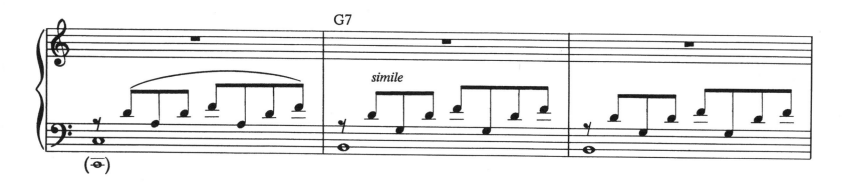

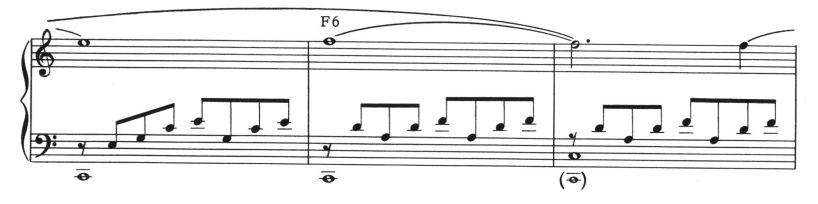

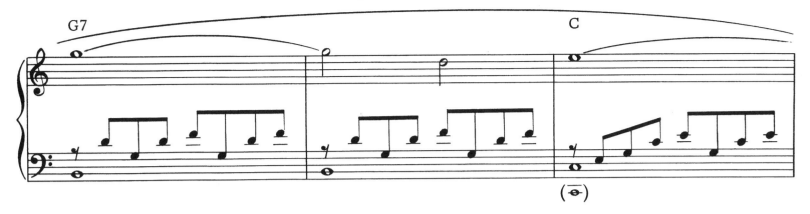

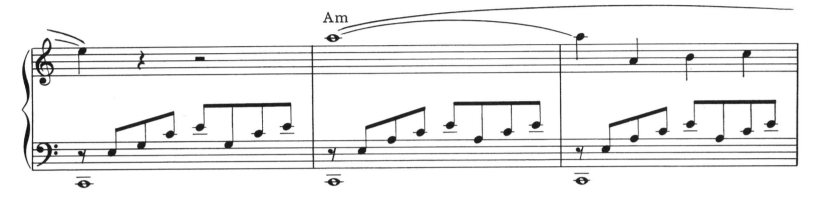

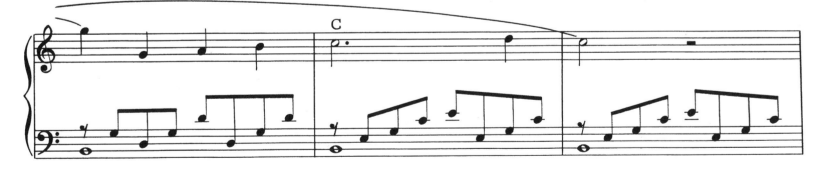

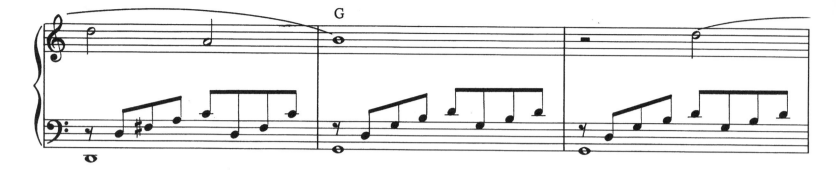

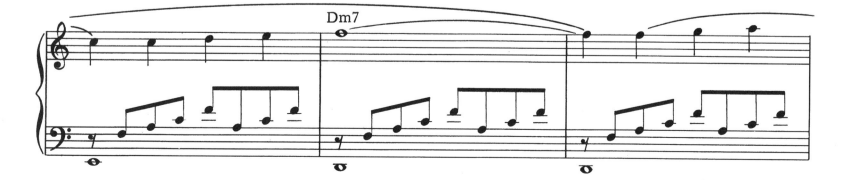

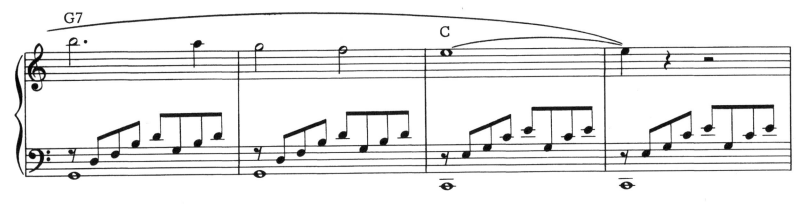

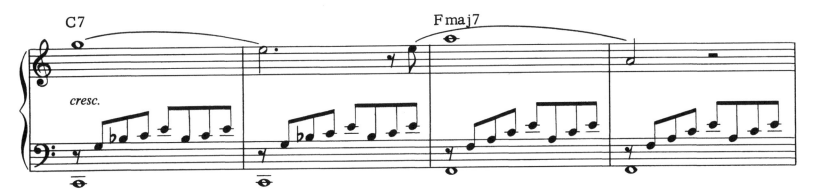

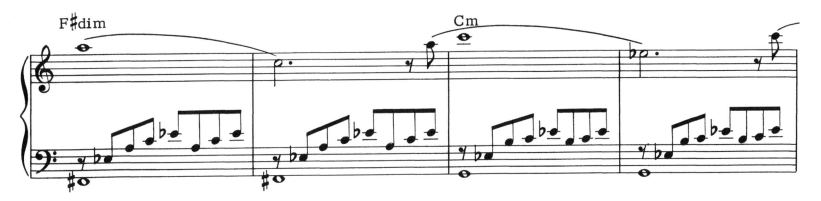

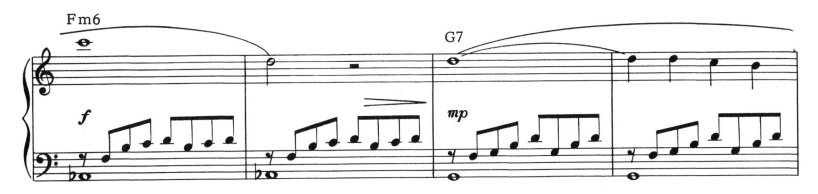

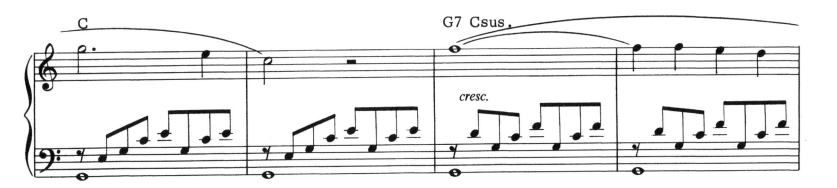

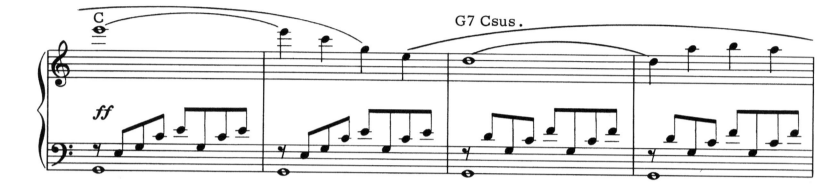

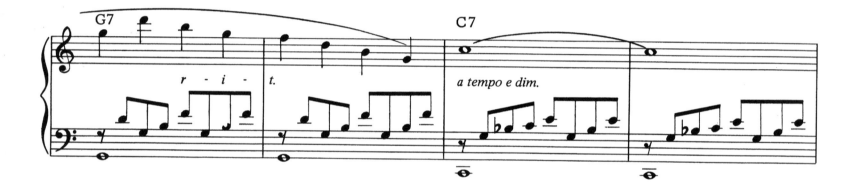

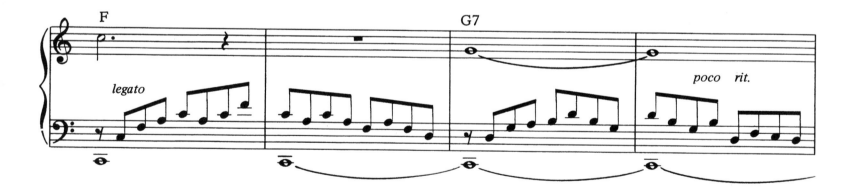

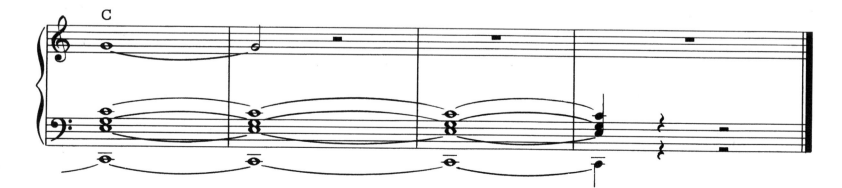

Canon in D

Electronic Organs
Upper: Tibias (Flutes) 16′, 4′
Lower: Diapason 8′, Melodia
Pedal: 16′
Vib./Trem.: On, Slow

Drawbar Organs
Upper: 800 6606 000
Lower: (00) 7310 000
Pedal: 55
Vib./Trem.: On, Slow

By JOHANN PACHELBEL

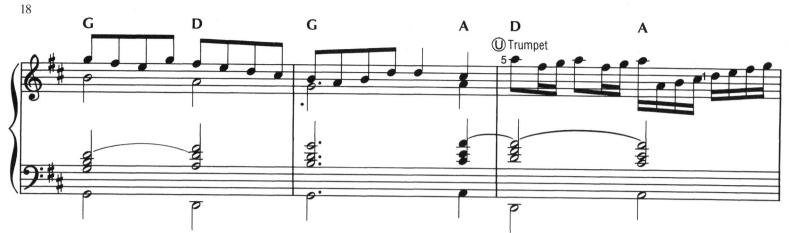

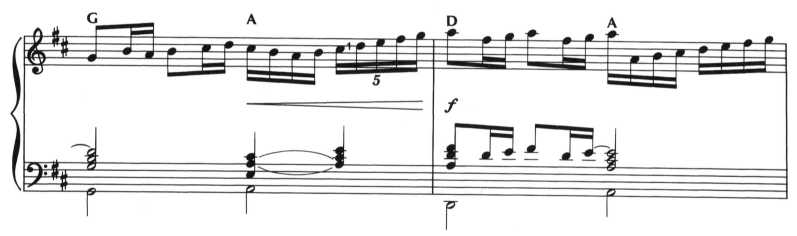

Ave Maria

Electronic and Pipe Organs

Upper:	Fls. 16' and 8', Horn 8', Clarinet 8'
Lower	Stgs. 8'
Pedal	Soft 16' to Gt.

Drawbar Organs

Upper:	42 6616 412 (00)
Lower:	(00) 5444 320 (0)
Pedal:	4 (0) 2 (0) (Spinet 3)

By FRANZ SCHUBERT

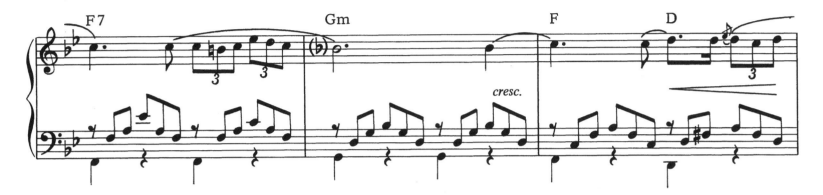

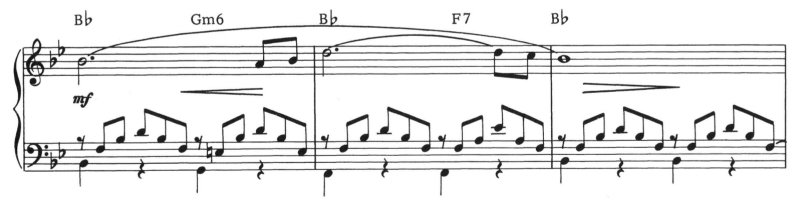

Because

Electronic Organs
Upper: Flutes (or Tibias) 16', 8', 4'
Lower: Melodia 8', Reed 8'
Pedal: 8'
Vib./Trem.: On, Slow

Drawbar Organs
Upper: 80 4804 000
Lower: (00) 7435 000
Pedal: 56
Vib./Trem.: On, Slow

Words by EDWARD TESCHEMACHER
Music by GUY D'HARDELOT

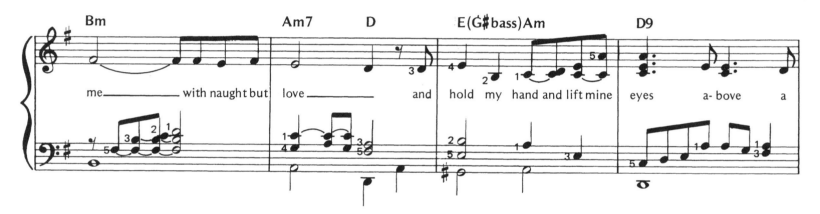

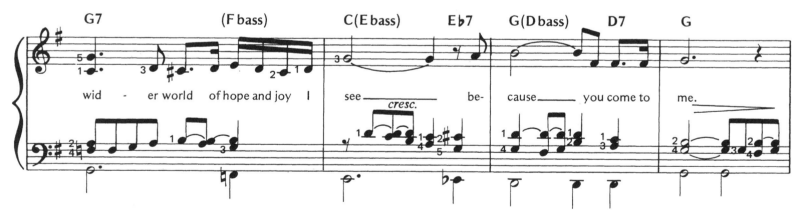

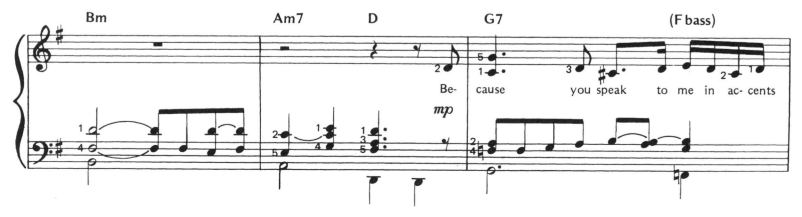

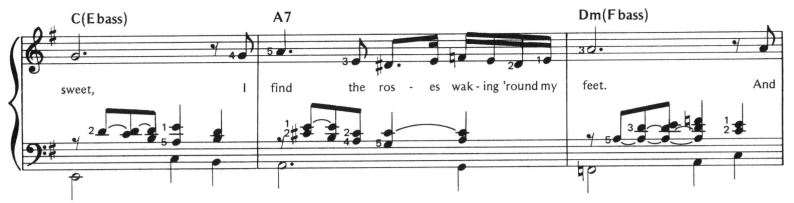

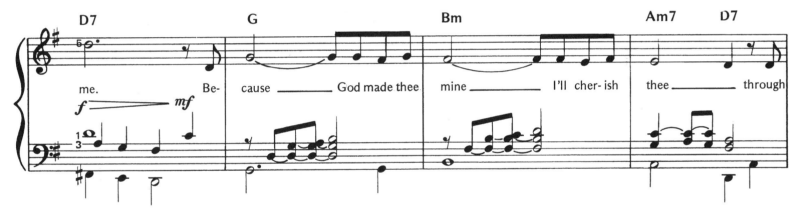

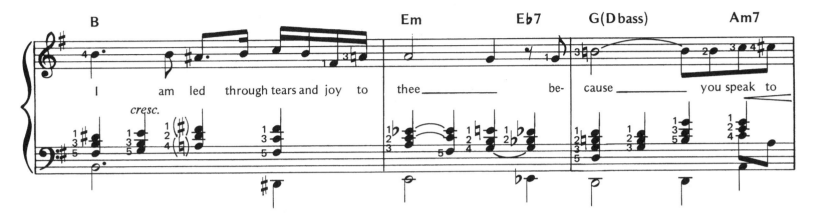

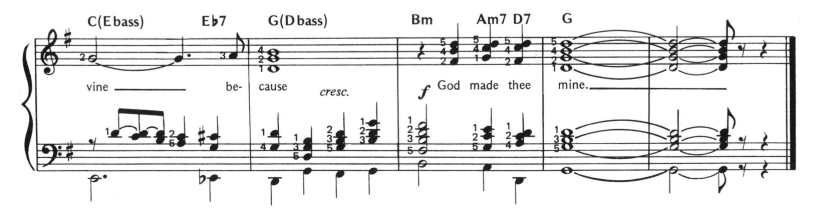

Bridal Chorus

from LOHENGRIN

*Electronic and Pipe Organs

Upper: 8' Stgs., Soft 8' and 4' Fls.
Lower: Stg. 8', Horn (Fl.) 8'
Pedal: Soft 16' to Sw.

*Drawbar Organs

Upper: 00 5576 321 (00)
Lower: (00) 8822 112 (0)
Pedal: 4 (0) 2 (0) (Spinet 3)

By RICHARD WAGNER

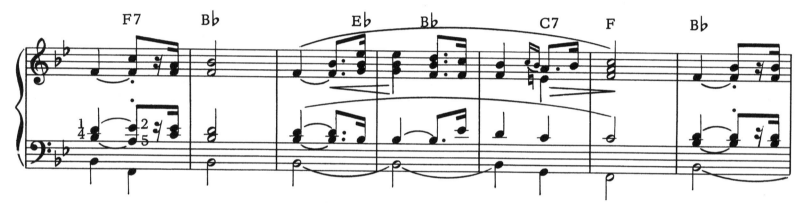

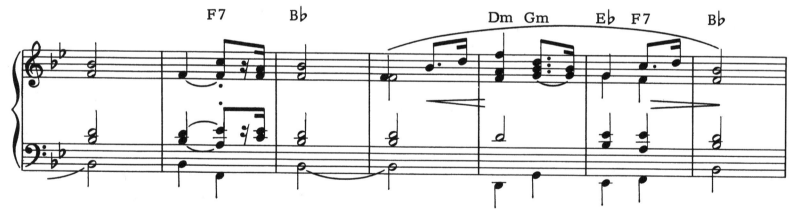

*Amount of Pedal Tone may be altered to suit room acoustics. Use of Vibrato and Reverberation is left to personal preference.
**Start at 𝄋 The first four measures are usually reserved for the entrance of the bride.

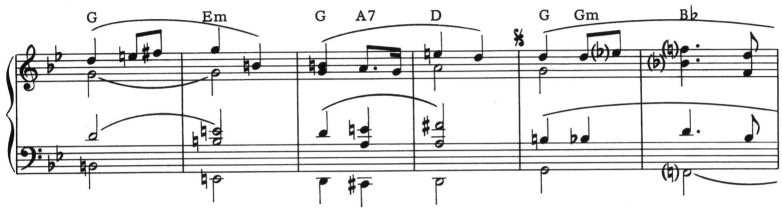

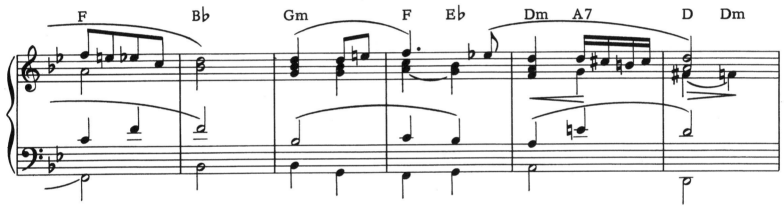

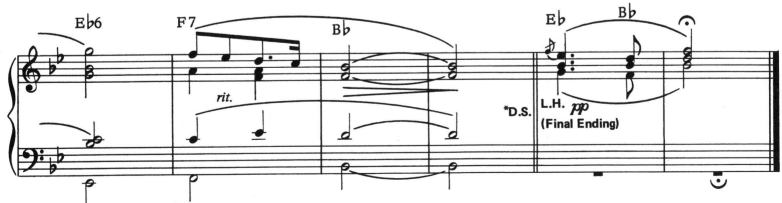

*D.S. to either of the three 𝄋 desired, or needed.

The Evening Star

from TANNHÄUSER

Electronic and Pipe Organs

Upper: Harp, or 8' Stgs. and Soft 16'
Lower: Trombone 8', Horn 8' (or Solo 8' Fl.)
Pedal: Soft 16'

Drawbar Organs

Upper: Harp, or Percussion,
         (Controls optional to balance) or
         42 6655 440 (00)
Lower: (00) 8862 000 (0)
Pedal: 4 (0) 2 (0) (Spinet 3)

By RICHARD WAGNER

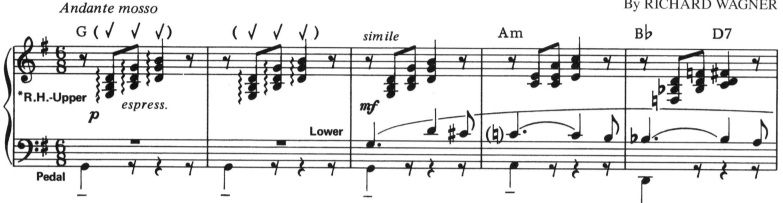

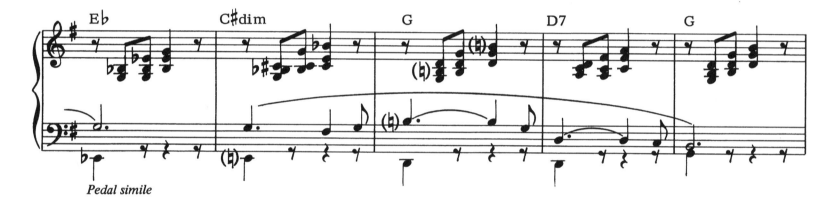

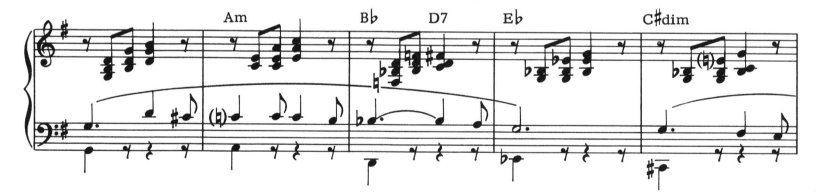

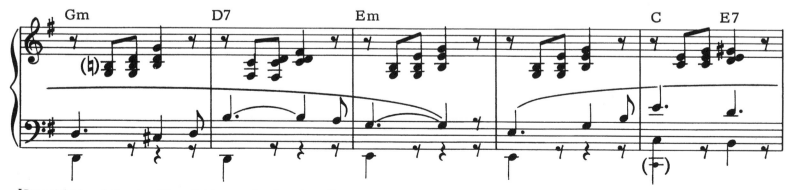

*Play right hand chords with a slight arpeggiando — harp-like.

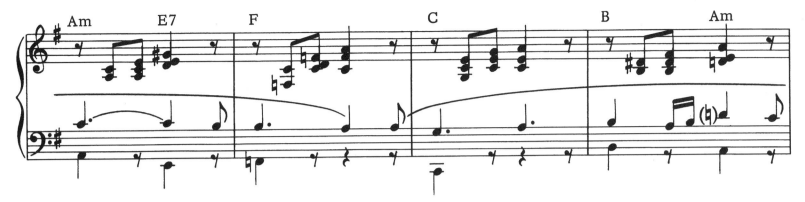

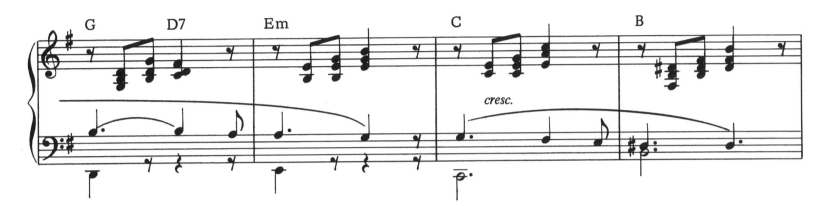

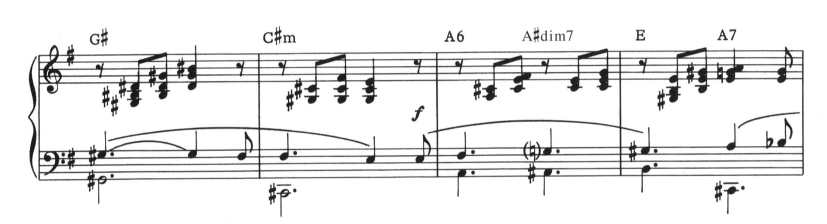

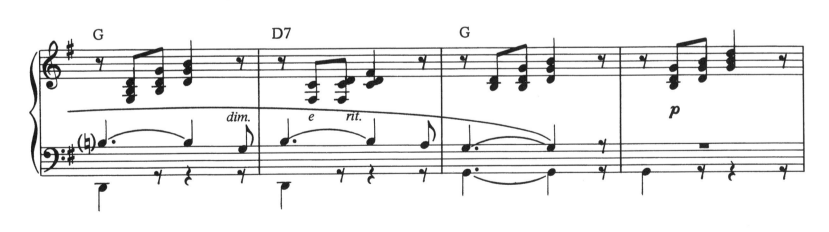

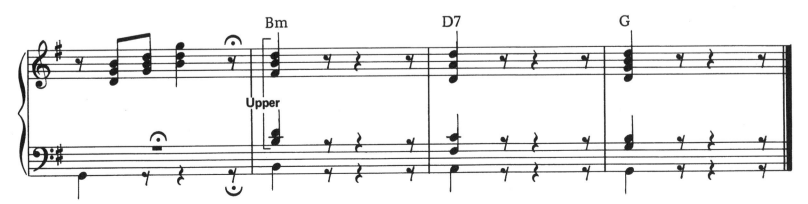

Gymnopédie No. 2

Upper: Flute (Tibia) 16', 8'
Diapason 8'
Lower: Melodia, Fr. Horn 8'
Pedal: 8', Medium
Vibrato: On

Upper: 40 6714 200
Lower: (00) 5523 540 (0)
Pedal: 4-3
Vib. & Cho: On, Normal

By ERIK SATIE

Lento e tristo

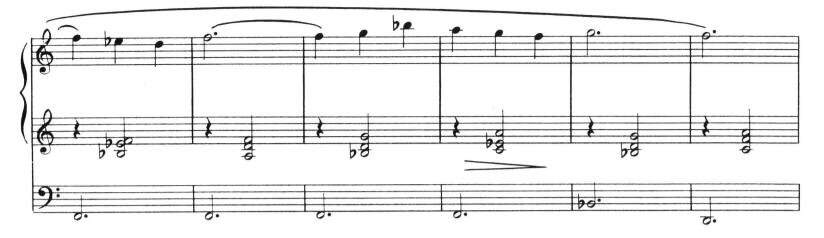

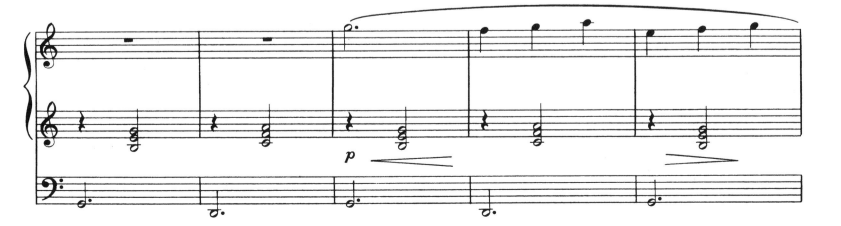

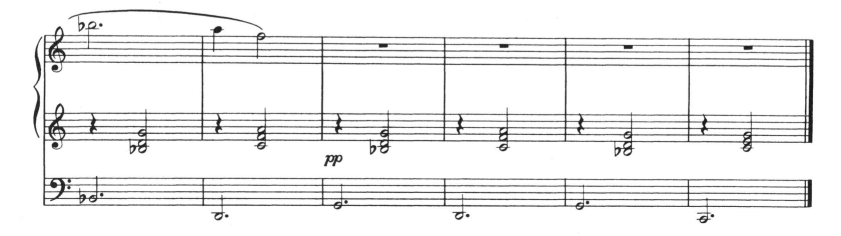

Jesu, Joy of Man's Desiring

Electronic and Pipe Organs

Upper:	Fr. Horn 8′ (Solo Fl. 8′)
Lower:	Soft 8′ and 4′ Stgs. and Fls.
Pedal:	Soft 16′ to Gt.

Drawbar Organs

Upper:	00 6060 000 (00)
Lower:	(00) 5332 321 (0)
Pedal:	4 (0) 2 (0) (Spinet 3)

By JOHANN SEBASTIAN BACH

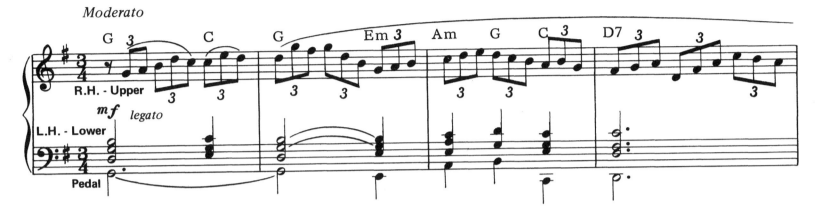

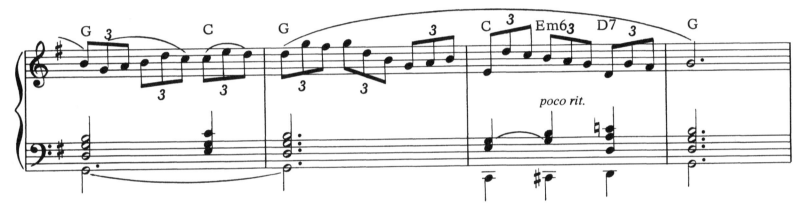

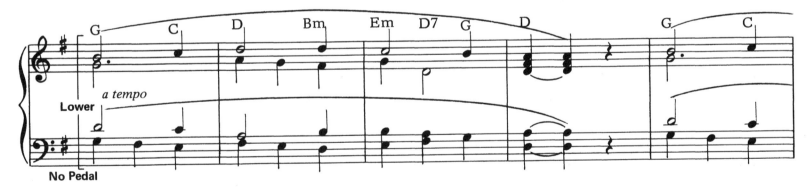

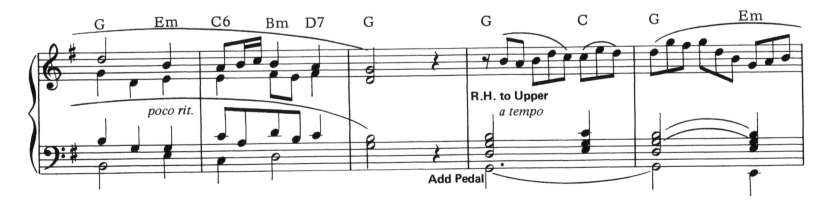

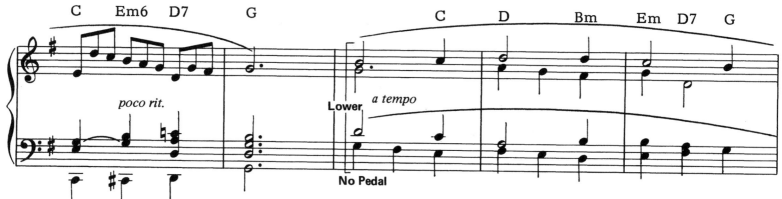

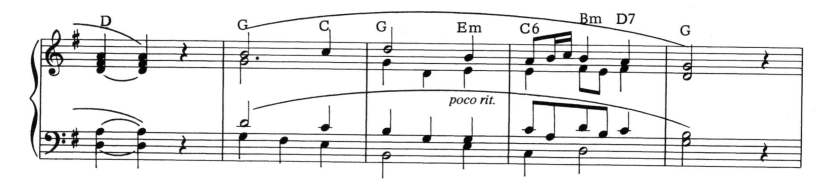

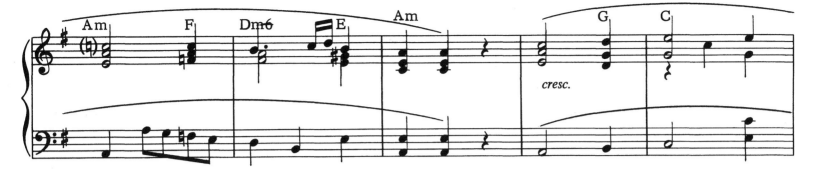

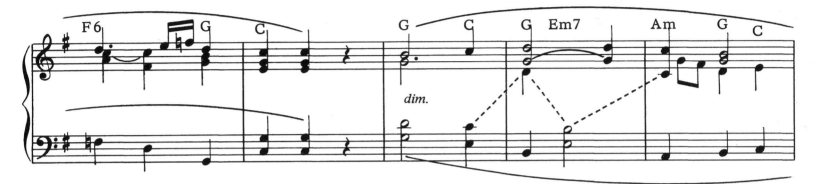

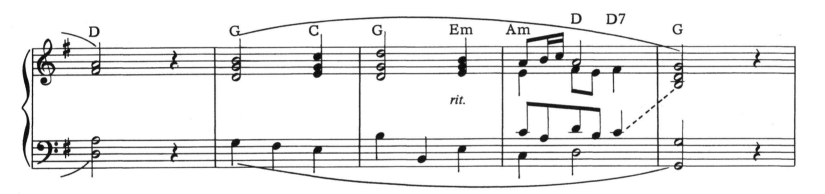

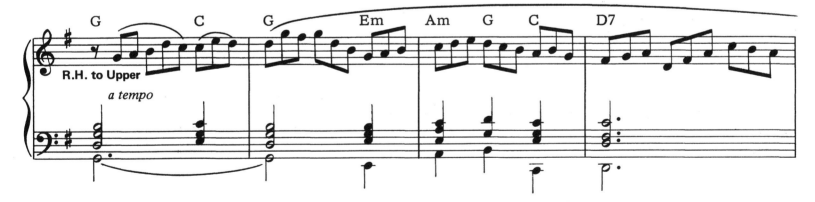

I Love You Truly

Upper: Flutes (or Tibias) 16', 8', 4'
Lower: Melodia 8', Reed 8'
Pedal: 8'
Vib./Trem.: On, Fast

Upper: 80 4800 000
Lower: (00) 7334 011
Pedal: 05
Vib./Trem.: On, Fast

Words and Music by
CARRIE JACOBS-BOND

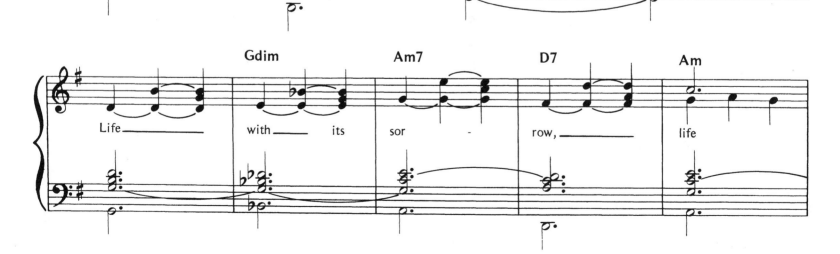

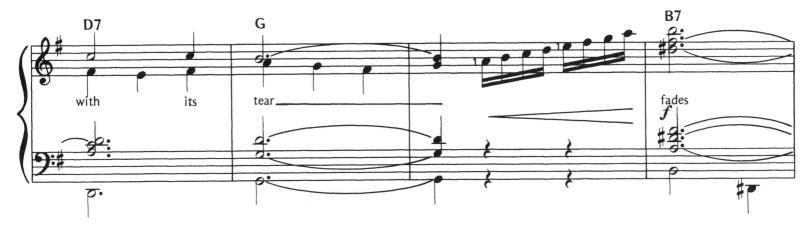

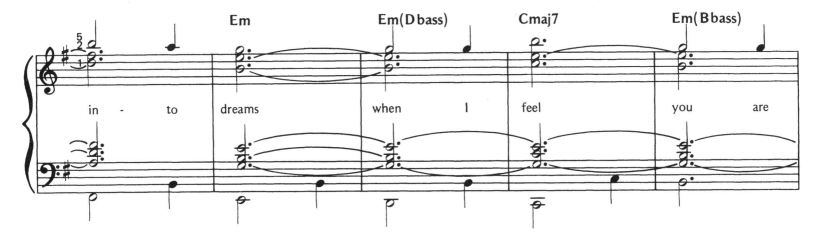

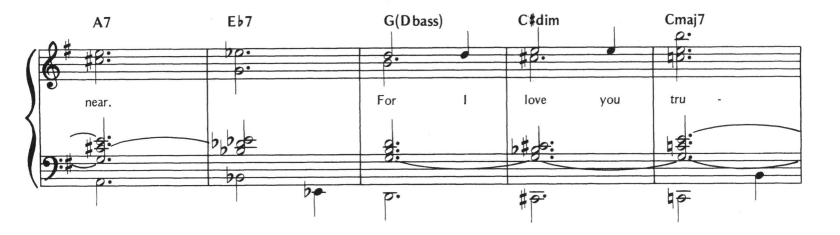

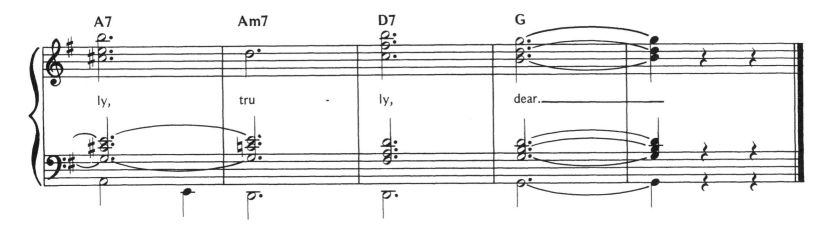

Ich Liebe Dich

(I Love Thee)

STANDARD ORGAN REGISTRATION

Upper: Flute (Tibia) 8'
        Trumpet, String 8'
Lower: String, Flute 8'
Pedal: 8', Medium
Vibrato: On, Light

DRAWBAR ORGAN REGISTRATION

Upper: 00 8836 321
Lower: (00) 5642 200 (0)
Pedal: 4-3
Vib. & Cho: On, Normal

Words and Music by
EDVARD GRIEG

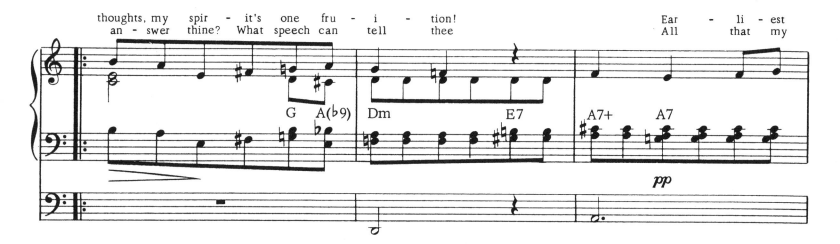

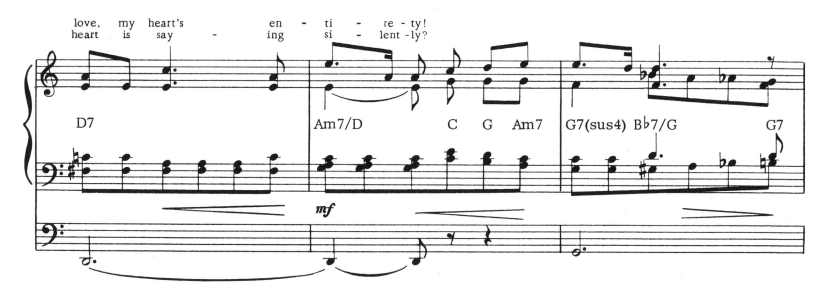

Jupiter
from THE PLANETS

Upper: *mf*
Lower: *p*
Pedal: *p*

By GUSTAV HOLST

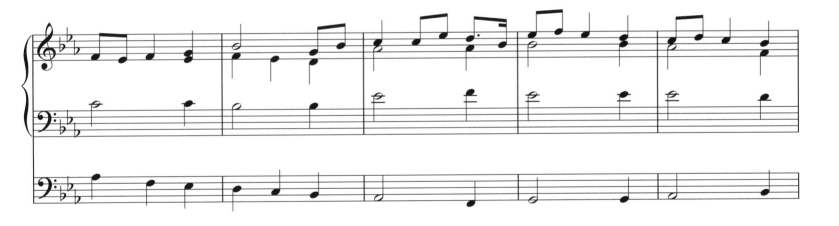

Meditation
from THAÏS

STANDARD ORGAN REGISTRATION

Upper:	Flutes (Tibia) 16', 8'
Lower:	Melodia 8'
Pedal:	16', Medium
Vibrato:	On, Normal

DRAWBAR ORGAN REGISTRATION

Upper:	40 8764 000
Lower:	(00) 6543 000(0)
Pedal:	5-3
Vibrato:	On, Normal

By JULES MASSENET

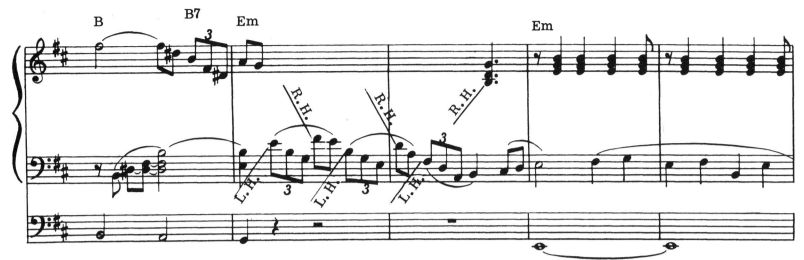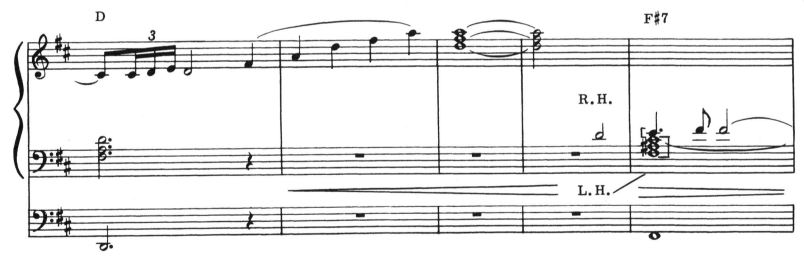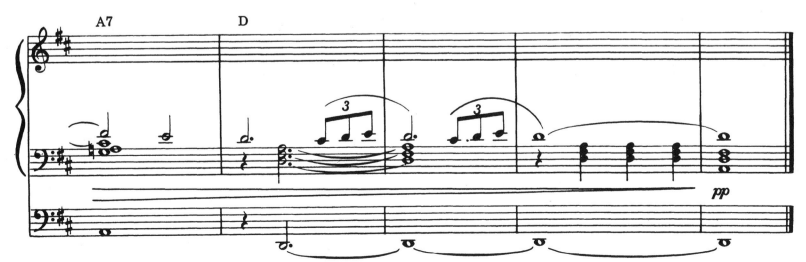

O Perfect Love

Electronic and Pipe Organs

Upper: Soft 8′ and 4′ Stgs. and Fls.
Lower: Fl. 8′ (Horn)
Pedal: Soft 16′ to Sw.

Drawbar Organs

Upper: 00 5332 221 (00)
Lower: (00) 6060 000 (0)
Pedal: 4 (0) 2 (0) (Spinet 3)

Words by DOROTHY FRANCES GURNEY
Music by JOSEPH BARNBY

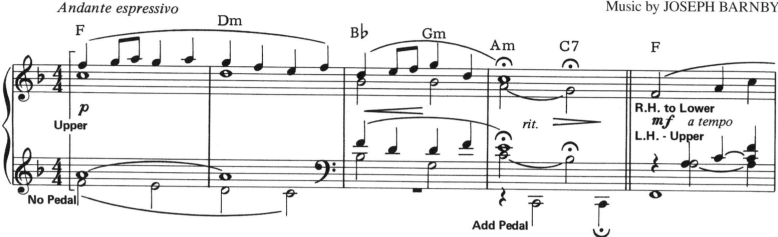

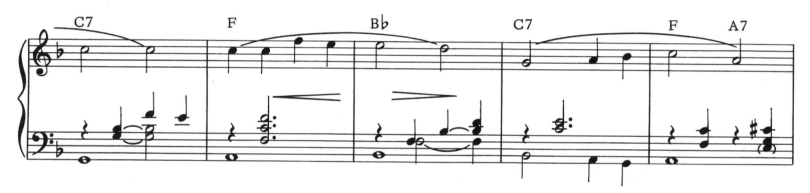

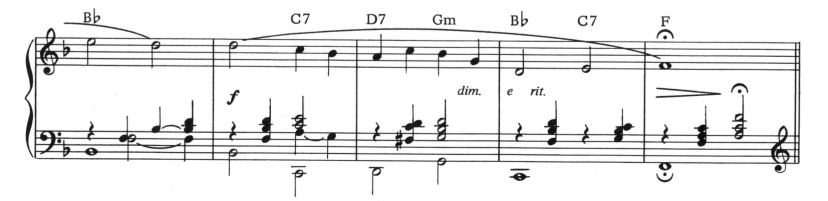

43

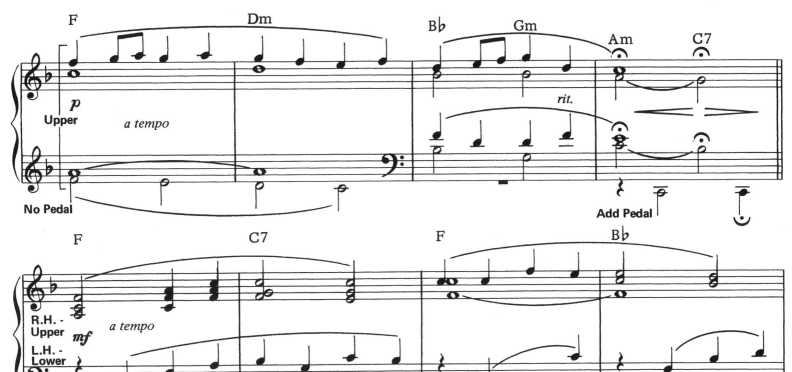

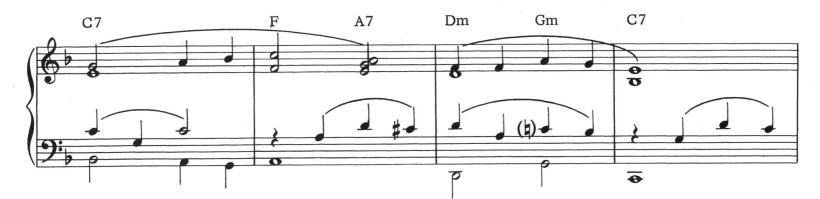

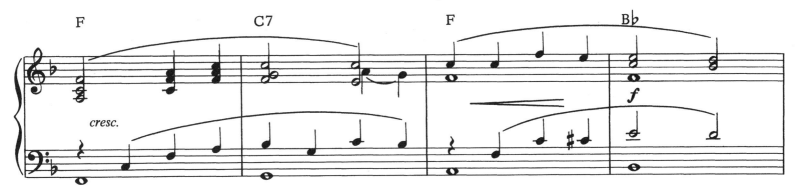

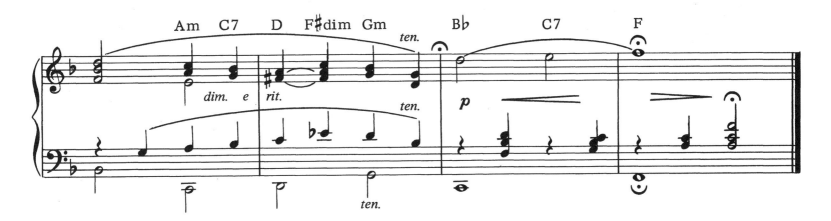

Ode to Joy

from SYMPHONY NO. 9 IN D MINOR, FOURTH MOVEMENT CHORAL THEME

Electronic Organs
Upper: Flutes (or Tibias) 16', 8', 4', 2'
Lower: Flutes 8', 4', Diapason 8'
Pedal: 8'
Vib./Trem.: Off

Drawbar Organs
Upper: 80 6606 000
Lower: (00) 8504 000
Pedal: 65
Vib./Trem.: Off

Words by HENRY VAN DYKE
Music by LUDWIG VAN BEETHOVEN

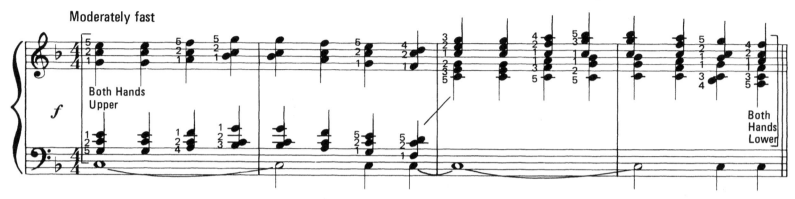

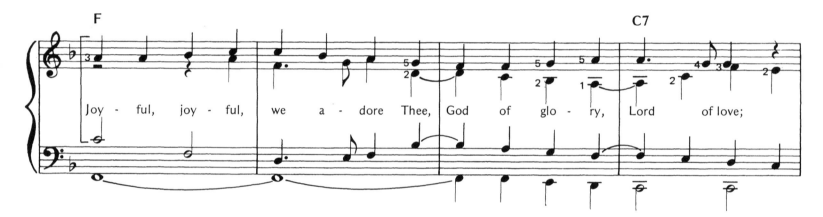

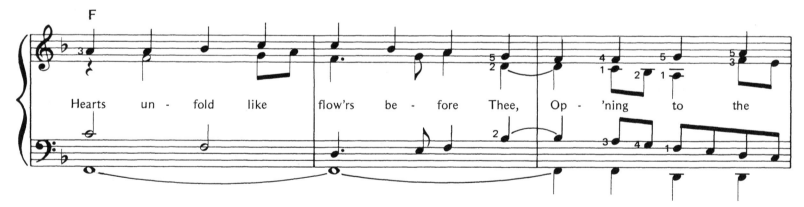

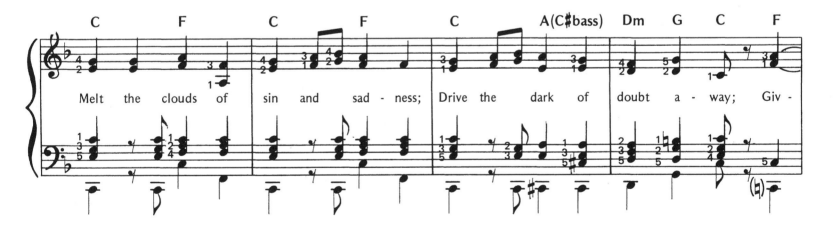

Oh, Promise Me

Electronic Organs
Upper: Flutes (or Tibias) 16', 8', 4'
Lower: Melodia 8', Reed 8'
Pedal: 8'
Vib./Trem.: On, Slow

Drawbar Organs
Upper: 80 4804 000
Lower: (00) 7345 000
Pedal: 56
Vib./Trem.: On, Slow

Words by CLEMENT SCOTT
Music by REGINALD DE KOVEN

Moderately flowing

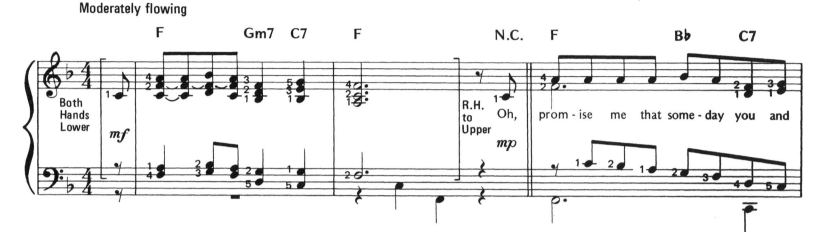

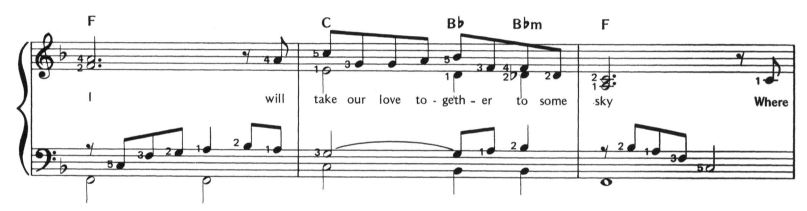

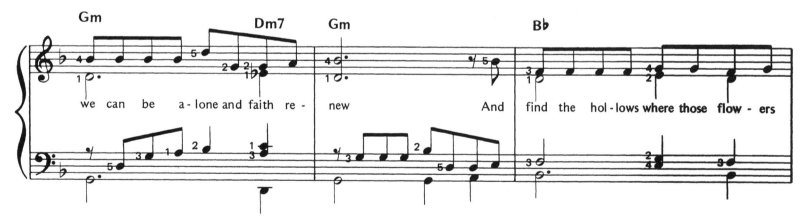

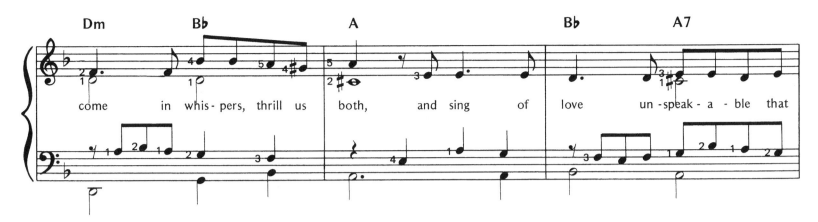

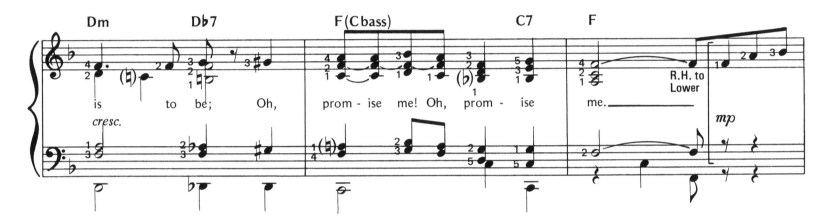

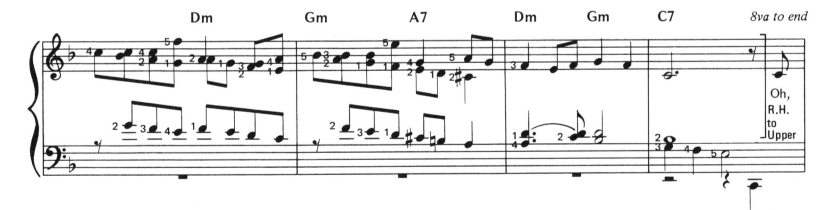

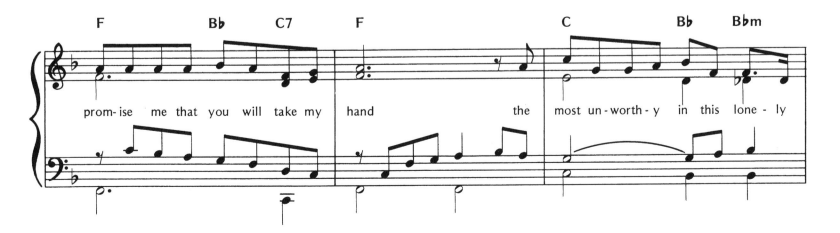

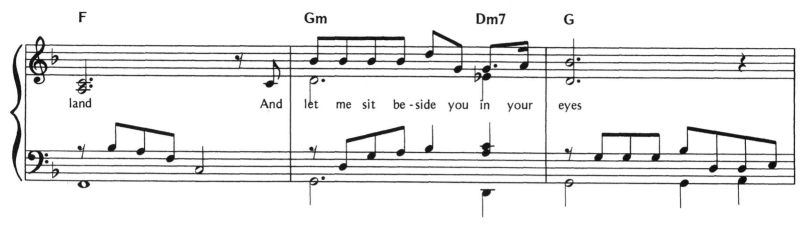

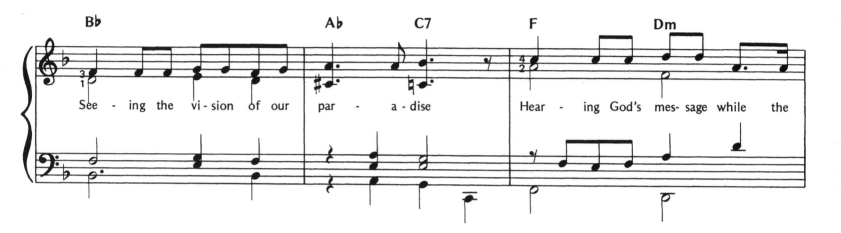

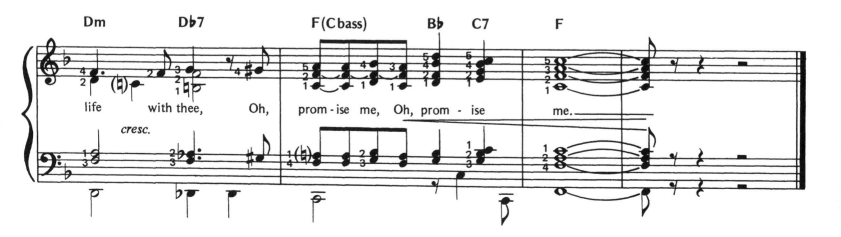

Panis angelicus
(O Lord Most Holy)

Upper: *mf*
Lower: *p*
Pedal: *p*

By CÉSAR FRANCK

50

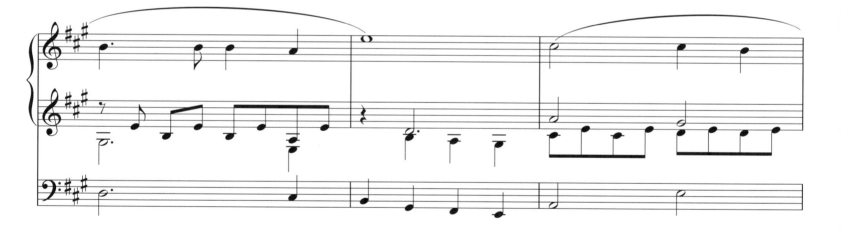

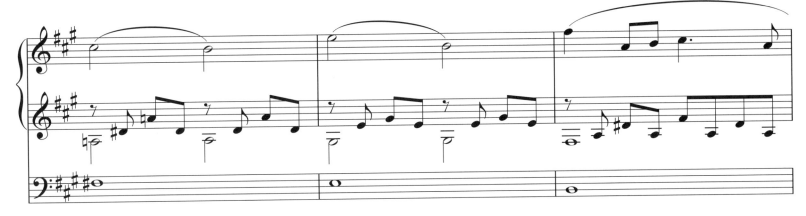

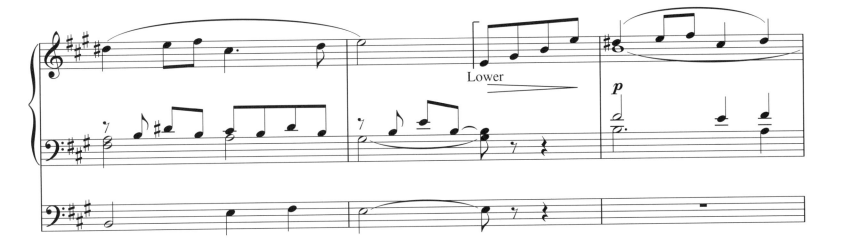

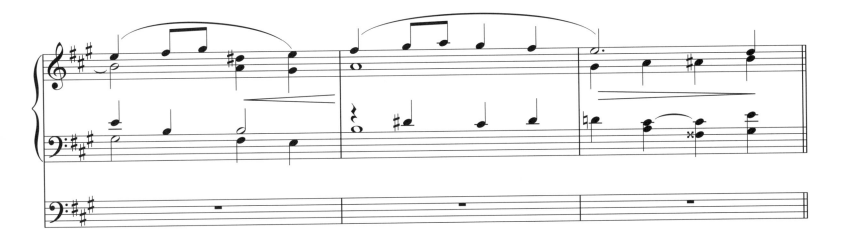

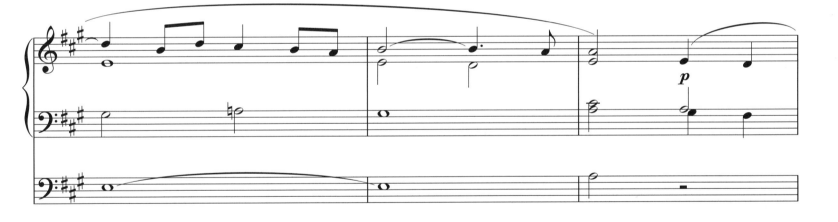

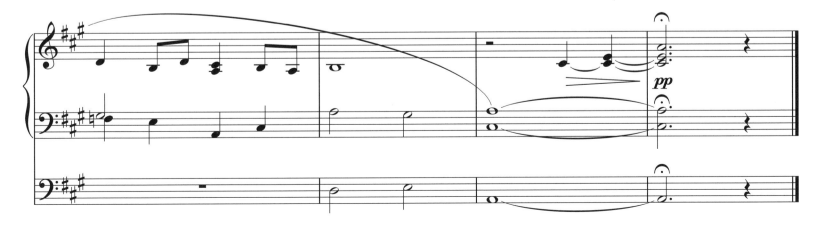

Piano Concerto No. 2
(Third Movement Excerpt)

STANDARD ORGAN REGISTRATION

Upper: English Horn (Reed) 8'
Lower: Viola (String) 8'
Pedal: 8', Medium
Vibrato: On, Normal

DRAWBAR ORGAN REGISTRATION

Upper: 00 6724 200
Lower: (00) 4544 000(0)
Pedal: 4-3
Vibrato: On, Normal

By SERGEI RACHMANINOFF

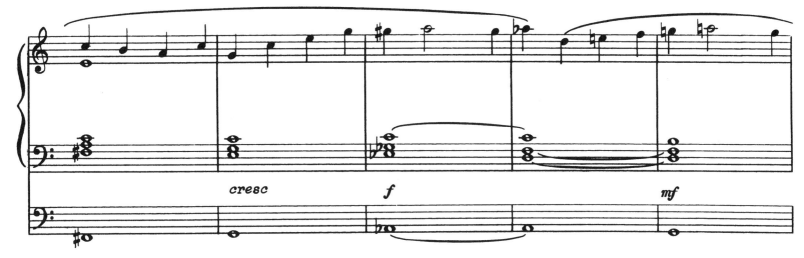

cresc   f   mf

dim

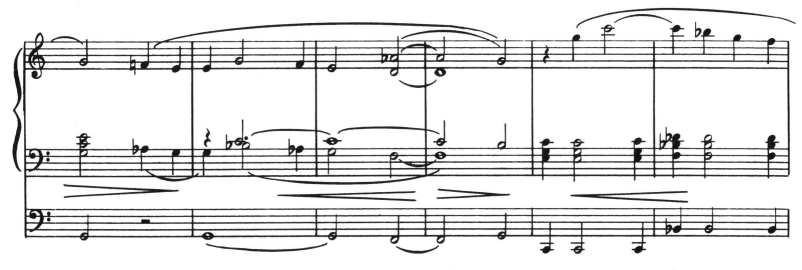

marc

Rondeau

Upper: **ff**
Lower: **f**
Pedal: **f**

By JEAN-JOSEPH MOURET

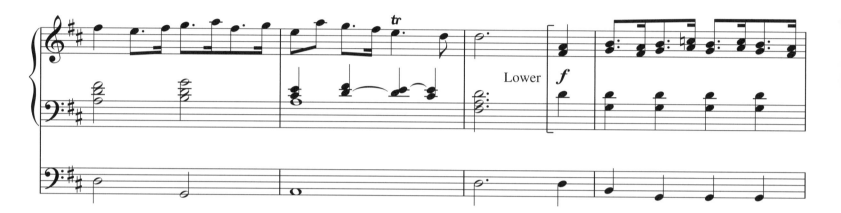

The Swan

(Le Cygne)

from CARNIVAL OF THE ANIMALS

STANDARD ORGAN REGISTRATION

Upper:	Flutes (Tibia) 16', 8'
Lower:	Diapason 8'
Pedal:	8', Medium
Vibrato:	On, Normal

DRAWBAR ORGAN REGISTRATION

Upper:	00 6775 440
Lower:	(00) 5664 220(0)
Pedal:	4–2
Vibrato:	On, Normal

By CAMILLE SAINT-SAËNS

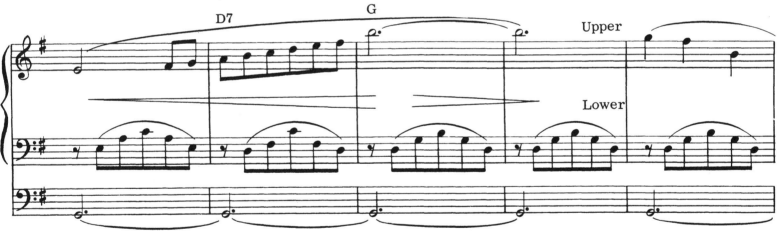

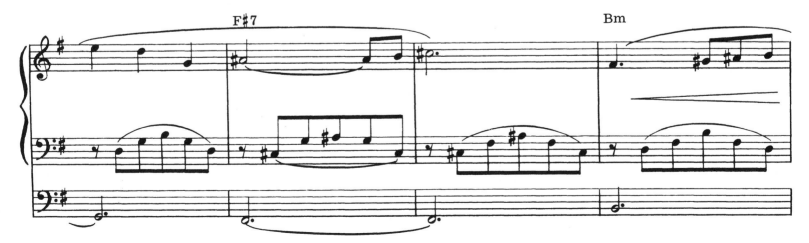

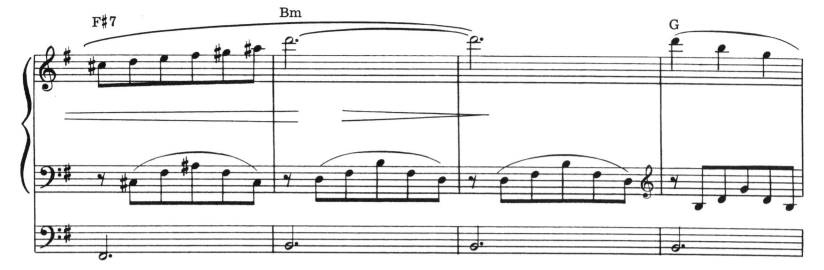

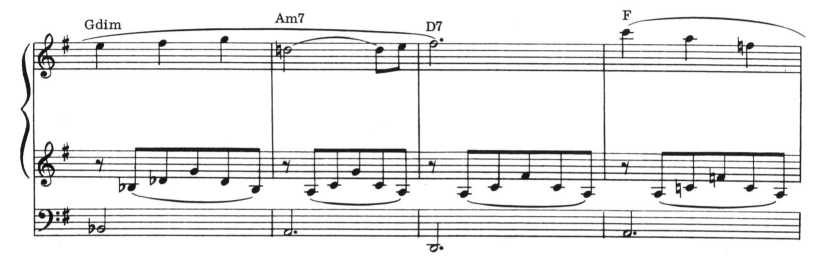

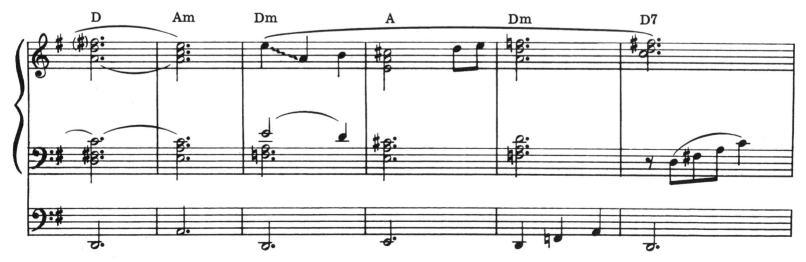

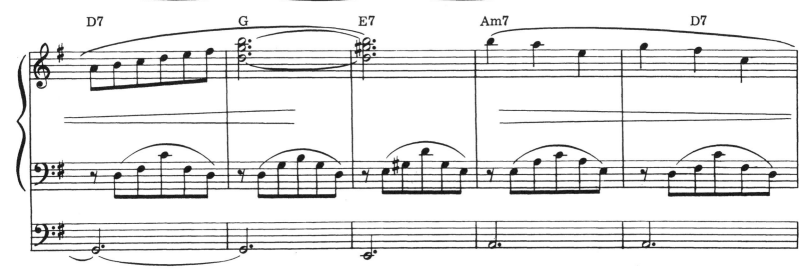

Serenade

(Ständchen)

STANDARD ORGAN REGISTRATION

Upper:	Diapason, Strings 8'
Lower:	Saxophone (Reed) 8'
Pedal:	16', Medium
Vibrato:	On, Normal

DRAWBAR ORGAN REGISTRATION

Upper:	30 7867 000
Lower:	(00) 5645 000(0)
Pedal:	4-2
Vibrato:	On, Normal

By FRANZ SCHUBERT

Sheep May Safely Graze

from CANTATA NO. 208

Electronic and Pipe Organs

Upper: 8' Stgs.
Lower: Solo Fl. 8' (Fr. Horn 8')
Pedal: Soft 16' to Sw.

Drawbar Organs

Upper: 00 6666 550 (00)
Lower: (00) 6404 000 (0)
Pedal: 4 (0) 2 (0) (Spinet 3)

By JOHANN SEBASTIAN BACH

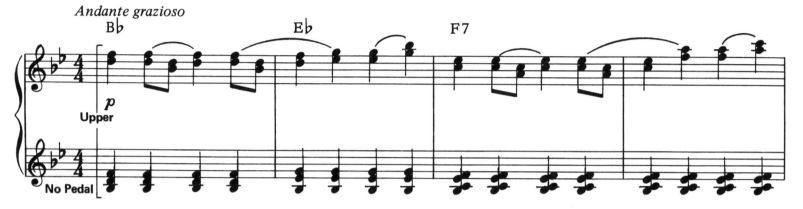

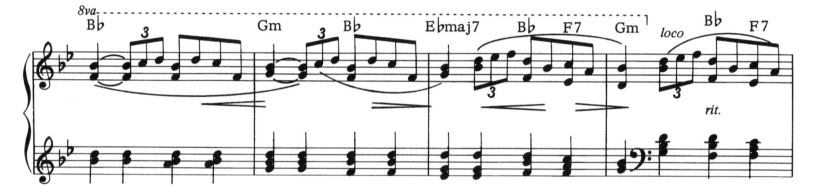

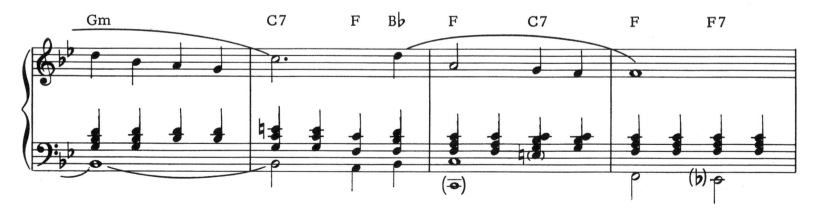

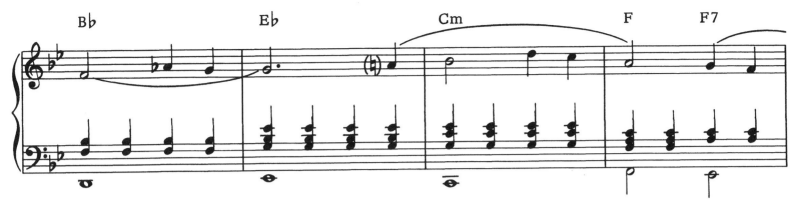
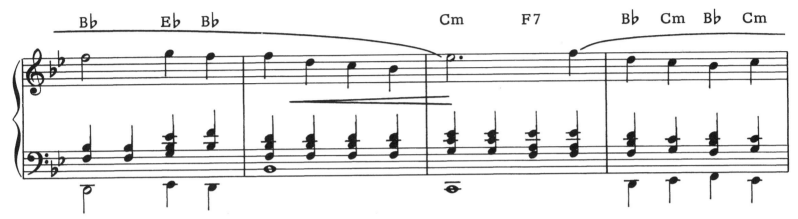
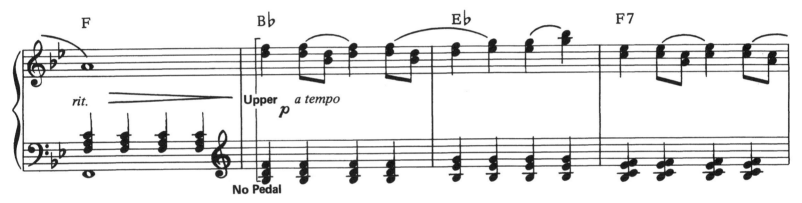
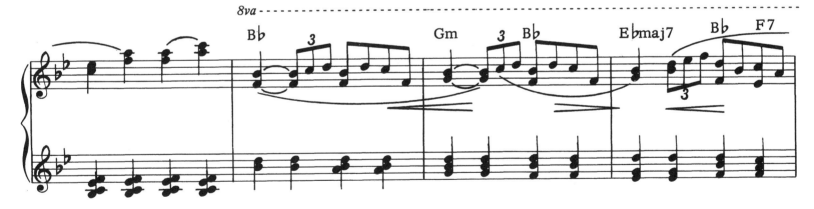
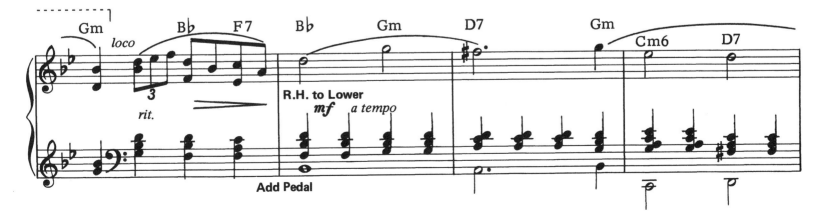

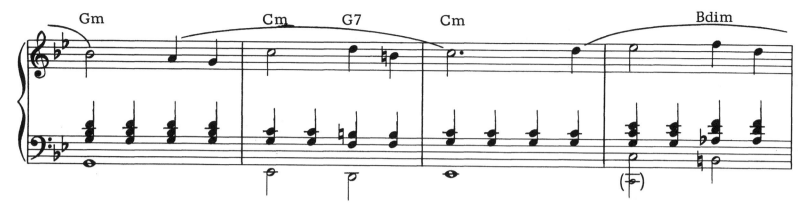

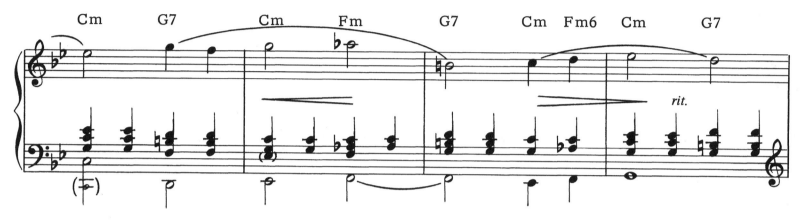

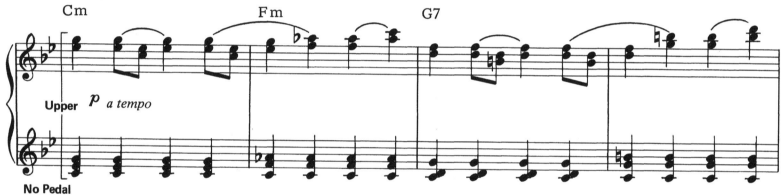

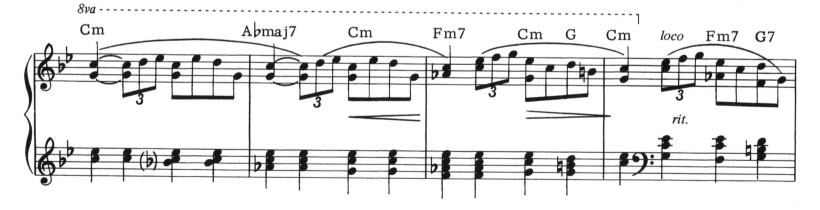

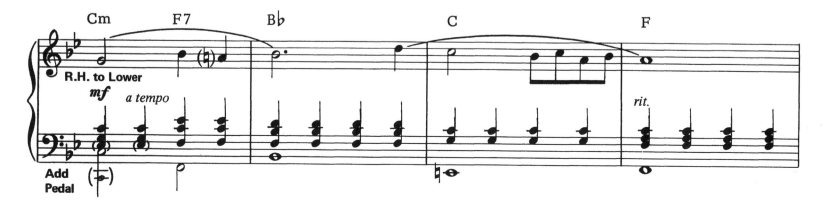

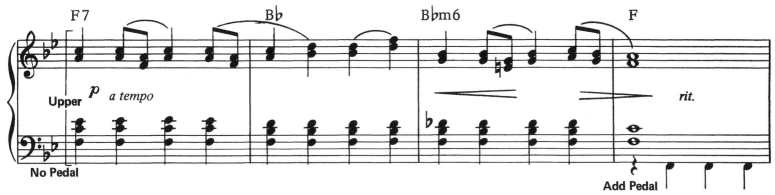

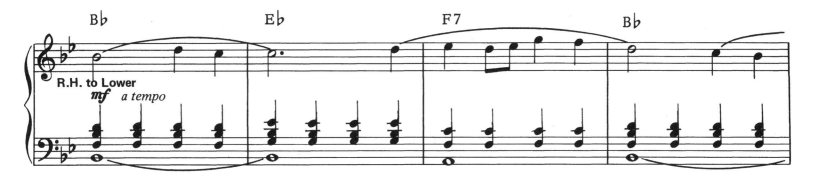

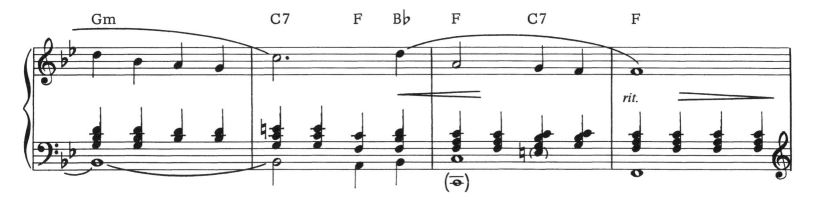

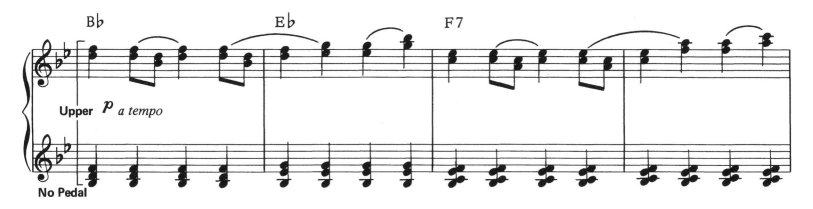

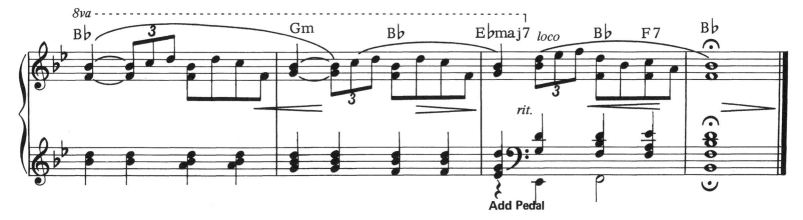

Sinfonia
from CANTATA NO. 156

STANDARD ORGAN REGISTRATION

Upper: Flute (Tibia) 8', 4'
String 8'
Lower: Melodia, Dulciana 8'
Pedal: 16', Medium
Vibrato: On, Light

DRAWBAR ORGAN REGISTRATION

Upper: 00 8776 432
Lower: (00) 7817 344 (0)
Pedal: 6-4
Vib. & Cho: Off

By JOHANN SEBASTIAN BACH

Original Ending   *Opt. D. C.* | *Opt. Ending*

Songs My Mother Taught Me

STANDARD ORGAN REGISTRATION

Upper:	Flutes (Tibia) 16', 8', 4'
	Strings 8'
Lower:	Diapason 8'
Pedal:	16', Medium
Vibrato:	On, Normal

DRAWBAR ORGAN REGISTRATION

Upper:	00 6526 214
Lower:	(00) 5535 000(0)
Pedal:	4-2
Vibrato:	On, Normal

By ANTONÍN DVOŘÁK

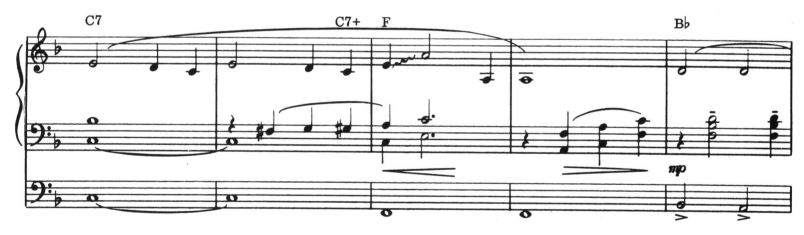

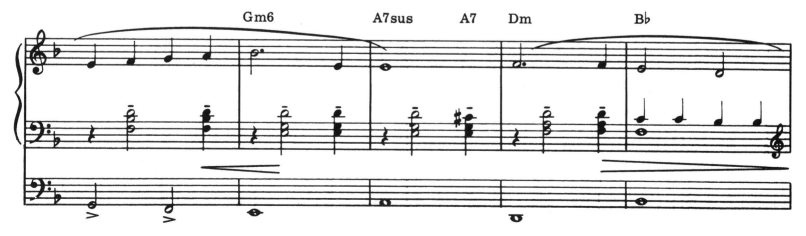

To a Wild Rose
from WOODLAND SKETCHES

STANDARD ORGAN REGISTRATION

Upper:	Strings 8'
Lower:	Flute 8'
Pedal:	8', Medium
Vibrato:	On, Normal

DRAWBAR ORGAN REGISTRATION

Upper:	00 6736 244
Lower:	(00) 4534 200(0)
Pedal:	4-2
Vibrato:	On, Normal

By EDWARD MacDOWELL

Andante

Trumpet Voluntary

Electronic and Pipe Organs

Upper: Trumpet 8', Stgs. 8', Fls. 8' and 4'
Lower: Horn 8', Stgs. 8' and 4' (Open Diap. 8' ad lib.)
Pedal: 16' and 8' to balance Gt. to Ped.

Drawbar Organs

Upper: 00 8887 650 (00)
Lower: (00) 6665 322 (0)
Pedal: 5 (0) 3 (0) (Spinet 4)

By JEREMIAH CLARKE

*Any of the sections may be repeated if desired.

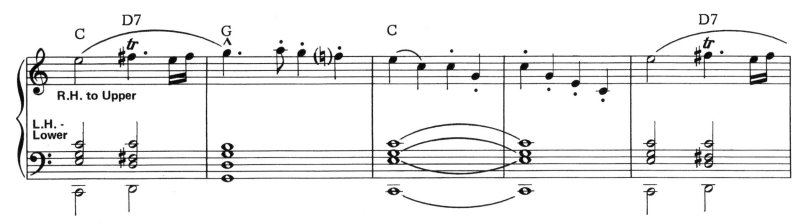

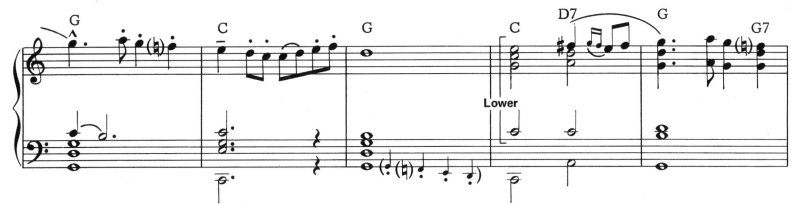

*This section may be repeated, if desired, an octave higher on the upper ad lib.

Wedding March

from A MIDSUMMER NIGHT'S DREAM

Electronic Organs

Upper: Flutes (or Tibias) 8', 4', 2'
        Diapason 8', String 8'
Lower: Flutes 8', 4', String 8'
Pedal: 16', 8'
Vib./Trem.: Off

Drawbar Organs

Upper: 00 8868 003
Lower: (00) 8806 001
Pedal: 86
Vib./Trem.: Off

By FELIX MENDELSSOHN

Majestically

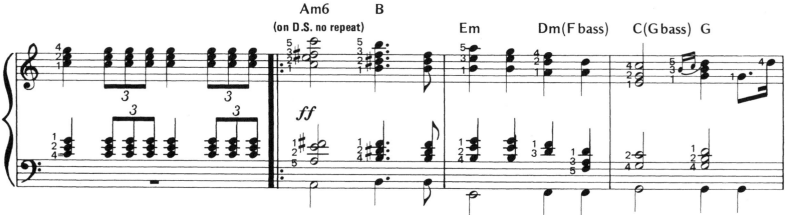

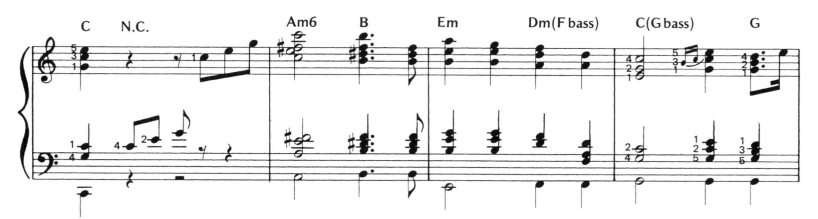

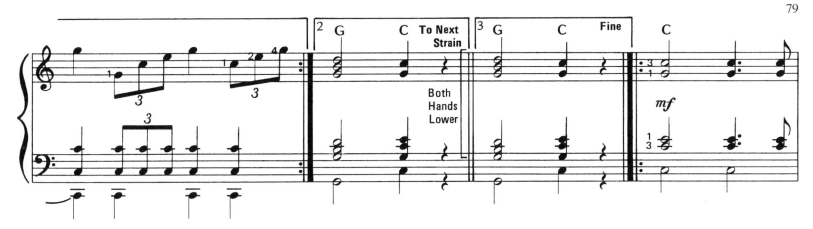

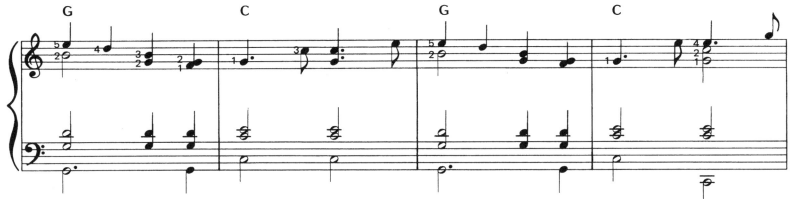

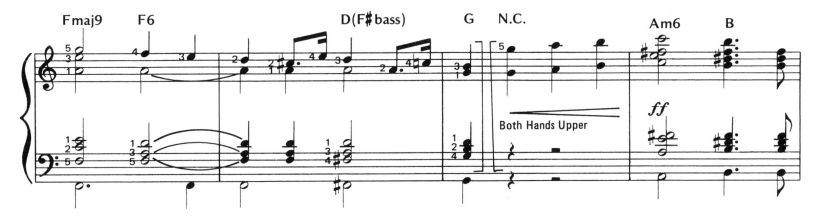

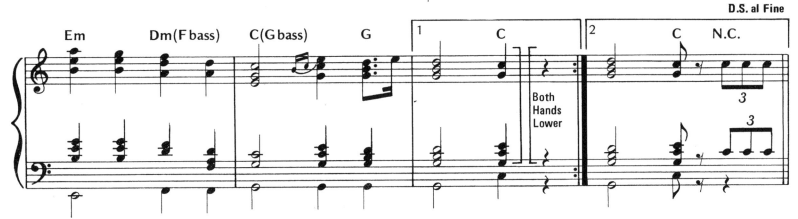

Trumpet Tune

Electronic Organs
Upper: Flutes (or Tibias) 16', 8', 4', 2',
       String 8', Trumpet
Lower: Flutes 8', 4', Reed 8'
Pedal: 16', 8'
Vib./Trem.: Off

Drawbar Organs
Upper: 80 8104 103
Lower: (00) 6403 004
Pedal: 65
Vib./Trem.: Off

By HENRY PURCELL

Stately